Sea Anemone

DOMINIQUE A. DIDIER

Published in the United States of America by Cherry Lake Publishing
Ann Arbor, Michigan
www.cherrylakepublishing.com

Consultants: Dominique A. Didier, PhD, Associate Professor, Department of Biology, Millersville University;
Marla Conn, ReadAbility, Inc.
Book design: Sleeping Bear Press

Photo Credits: ©Michael Klenetsky/Thinkstock, cover, 1, 25; ©Rich Carey/Shutterstock Images, 5, 18; ©Aleksey
Stemmer/Shutterstock Images, 7; ©b_ial_y/Thinkstock, 9; ©Dorling Kindersley/Thinkstock, 10, 22; ©Jupiterimages/
Thinkstock, 11; ©Reto Kunz/Thinkstock, 12; ©Kelpfish/Dreamstime.com, 15; ©Lokibaho/iStock, 17; ©ifish/iStock, 19;
©Feng Yu/Dreamstime.com, 21; ©Aneese/Thinkstock, 26; ©Divehive/Dreamstime.com, 27; ©BrendanHunter/iStock, 29

Library of Congress Cataloging-in-Publication Data

Didier, Dominique A., author.
Sea anemone / by Dominique A. Didier.
     pages cm. — (Exploring our oceans)
  Summary: "Discover facts about sea anemones, including physical features, habitat, life cycle, food,
and threats to these ocean creatures. Photos, captions, and keywords supplement the narrative of
this informational text"—Provided by publisher.
  Audience: Age 8-12.
  Audience: Grades 4 to 6.
  Includes bibliographical references and index.
  ISBN 978-1-63188-022-3 (hardcover)—ISBN 978-1-63188-065-0 (pbk.)— ISBN 978-1-63188-108-4 (pdf)—
ISBN 978-1-63188-151-0 (ebook) 1. Sea anemones—Juvenile literature. I. Title. II. Title: Sea anemone.
III. Series: 21st century skills library. Exploring our oceans.

QL377.C7D53 2015
593.6—dc23   2014005275

Cherry Lake Publishing would like to acknowledge the work of
The Partnership for 21st Century Skills. Please visit www.p21.org
for more information.

Printed in the United States of America
Corporate Graphics Inc.

ABOUT THE AUTHOR

Dominique A. Didier has a doctoral degree in zoology. She teaches marine biology, ichthyology,
and zoology at Millersville University of Pennsylvania. When she's not teaching, she visits the
fish and marine creatures she loves, and enjoys snorkeling and scuba diving with her husband and
two children.

TABLE OF CONTENTS

UNDERWATER FLOWER?

The two swimmers put on their masks and snorkels and swam out through the clear, shallow tropical waters. Small, bright-colored fish darted around them. Most amazing of all was a beautiful flower waving back and forth in the gentle currents. But flowers don't grow underwater! They looked again, and the flower curled up. This was not a plant after all. It was a sea anemone.

A sea anemone is an animal. It is shaped like a **cylinder**. It has a short, thick stump with a crown of **tentacles** around the top. Most sea anemones are brightly colored. Their shape and colors make them look like large flowers. They belong to a class of animals known as anthozoans. In fact, the word *anthozoa* means "flower animals."

Sea anemones look a lot like flowers, but they're actually a type of animal.

The sea anemone lives in all oceans around the world. Most sea anemones live in shallow coastal water up to 164 feet (50 m) deep. Not all sea anemones are found in shallow water, though. They can live at all water depths. Some even live deeper than 32,800 feet (9,997 m). Scientists estimate that there are about 1,200 different species of sea anemones.

Sea anemones are closely related to the reef-building hard corals. They are also related to soft corals like sea fans. Unlike corals, which are **colonial** animals, the sea anemone is a solitary creature. Although they may occur in groups, each sea anemone is separate from the others.

Most sea anemones stay attached to the **substrate**, but they are able to move. One way sea anemones can move is by gliding along the bottom of the ocean. Some sea anemones can flex their bodies and swim short distances. There are even a few **pelagic** species that float.

LOOK AGAIN

LOOK CLOSELY AT THIS PHOTOGRAPH OF A SEA ANEMONE. WHAT FEATURES OF THE SEA ANEMONE MAKE IT SEEM MORE LIKE A FLOWER THAN AN ANIMAL?

SPECTACULAR TENTACLES

The sea anemone's tentacles surround an opening that leads into the gut of the creature. This single opening serves as both the mouth and the **anus** of the animal. Yes, food and waste go in and out of the same opening. YUK!

Most sea anemones are not very big. The base usually ranges from less than 0.25 inch (0.5 cm) to about 4 inches (10 cm) in diameter. But there are bigger ones. Some sea anemones are more than 5 feet (1.5 m) in diameter. Most are only a few inches tall, but a few can stretch to nearly 3 feet (1 m) tall.

[21ST CENTURY SKILLS LIBRARY]

Sea anemones come in all shapes, sizes, and colors.

BODY DIAGRAM

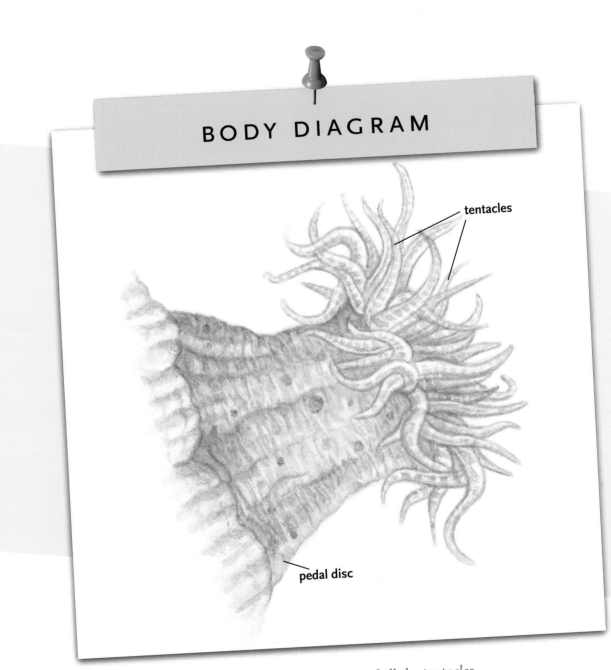

tentacles

pedal disc

The mouth is in the center of all the tentacles.

[21ST CENTURY SKILLS LIBRARY]

This white-spotted rose anemone has pulled its tentacles in to protect itself.

The sea anemone does not have a skeleton. Its thick base is very muscular and filled with fluid. When threatened, many sea anemones can contract their muscles to pull the tentacles and body inward to form a tight ball.

The tentacles are the most spectacular feature of the sea anemone. There can be one or more rings of tentacles that surround the mouth. Some sea anemones have long, slender, threadlike tentacles. Others have stout tentacles like strands of thick spaghetti. In some sea anemones, the tentacles are short and stubby. The tentacles often have bright colors and patterns.

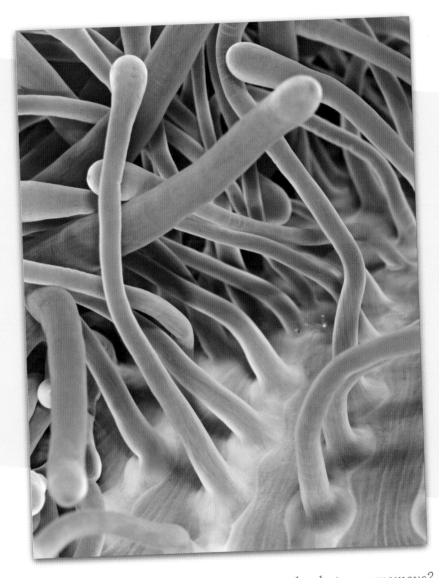

Why do you think the sea anemone has tentacles that are venomous?

[21ST CENTURY SKILLS LIBRARY]

What makes the tentacles of the sea anemone so special is that they contain unique stinging cells. These special cells contain a **nematocyst**. One end of it has **venomous** spines, and the other end is attached to the tentacle by a slender thread. The outside of the nematocyst has a **sensory** hair.

When something touches the sea anemone, the sensory hair is triggered and the nematocyst will shoot out. The venom of most anemones is not harmful to humans. A few sea anemones are very toxic. Their sting can cause great pain, even death. It is best to look, but don't touch, when you see a sea anemone.

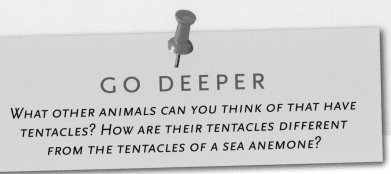

GO DEEPER

WHAT OTHER ANIMALS CAN YOU THINK OF THAT HAVE TENTACLES? HOW ARE THEIR TENTACLES DIFFERENT FROM THE TENTACLES OF A SEA ANEMONE?

FOOD AND FRIENDS

The sea anemone is a **carnivore**. Sea anemones eat a variety of foods, including fish, crabs, shrimp, mussels, and small **plankton**. They use their stinging tentacles to capture their food. Like a bullet, the nematocyst travels more than 6.5 feet (2 m) per second. It penetrates the prey and paralyzes it with toxin. Then the prey is wrapped by the anemone's tentacles, which bend inward and bring the prey to the mouth.

Food is drawn into the central cavity inside the base of the anemone. This central cavity is where digestion

Tentacles help the sea anemone bring its prey to its mouth.

takes place. All of the digested food is absorbed into the cells of the body. Waste materials will be mixed with the water inside this cavity and then pushed back out the mouth.

Sea anemones can feed in three different ways. They can actively capture their prey with their tentacles. Another method is to filter floating food particles as they land on the tentacles. Sea anemones can also capture food that has been released by wave action or other predators. The amount and type of food captured depends on the number and size of an anemone's tentacles.

Sea anemones have another way to obtain nutrition. They house algae inside their tissues. Like all plants, the algae uses sunlight to produce food through photosynthesis. This relationship benefits both the algae and the anemone. The algae are protected by the anemone and the anemone can obtain nutrients from photosynthesis by the algae.

The diet of a sea anemone includes fish and shrimp.

Living in a sea anemone protects clownfish from predators.

Sea anemones have an interesting relationship with clownfish. The clownfish has protective mucus that prevents it from being stung by the nematocysts. Protected from predators, the clownfish live in the anemones. The clownfish chases away other fish that may try to eat the anemone.

Sea anemones also have an interesting partnership with snails. Some sea anemones will hitch a ride on a snail. The anemone can offer the snail protection from predators. The anemone benefits by having free transportation to areas where food is available. The snail also provides a way for the anemone to escape its predators. This doesn't only happen with snails. Sometimes the sea anemone will attach to a hermit crab shell. 🐟

Sea anemones like to hitch a ride on hermit crabs and snails.

LOOK AGAIN

LOOK CLOSELY AT THIS PHOTOGRAPH OF THE SEA ANEMONE AND HERMIT CRAB. AFTER READING THIS CHAPTER, CAN YOU EXPLAIN THE HELPFUL RELATIONSHIP BETWEEN A SEA ANEMONE AND A HERMIT CRAB?

Many Ways to Make Babies

Where do baby sea anemones come from? And how can you tell a male sea anemone from a female? First, there is no way to tell the males and females apart. Sometimes the same anemone produces both eggs and **sperm**!

Sea anemones can reproduce in several ways. One way is by splitting apart. A single anemone can split in half and form two anemones. Instead of splitting completely, some sea anemones grow smaller baby anemones on the side of their base. New anemones are also formed when small pieces break off the bottom of the anemone's base.

It is impossible to tell the difference between male and female sea anemones.

Sea anemones reproduce in different ways than most sea creatures.

LOOK AGAIN

LOOK CLOSELY AT THIS PHOTOGRAPH OF AN ANEMONE. WHAT TYPE OF REPRODUCTION IS SHOWN IN THIS PHOTO?

Yet another way that sea anemones reproduce is by **shedding** eggs and sperm into the water. The egg and sperm will meet and form a planula larva. The planula larva is a very tiny organism covered in fine hairs called cilia. The cilia are like tiny oars that beat back and forth. The planula larva can move using its cilia. This larva will eventually develop into an adult anemone.

What is amazing is that most sea anemones don't stick to just one type of reproduction. Sea anemones will reproduce by splitting, budding, or by producing eggs and sperm.

A CHANGING OCEAN

The nematocysts of a sea anemone are a good defense. But they are not enough to ward off all predators. Many animals will attack and eat anemones, such as sea stars, sea spiders, snails, fish, and **nudibranchs**. These predators are often very specific. One predator species will attack only one particular species of sea anemone.

Sea anemones are not endangered. They are not good to eat, so there is no concern about humans overfishing them. Only one species is eaten as a delicacy, by people in southern Italy and Spain.

In addition to helping them catch prey, a sea anemone's venom also protects it against predators.

However, the main threat to sea anemones is humans. Large numbers of sea anemones are collected in the wild and sold in pet stores around the world. When anemones are removed from the wild, the animals that depend on them are affected.

Many people like to keep sea anemones in their saltwater fish tanks.

[21ST CENTURY SKILLS LIBRARY]

These sea anemones and clownfish have made a home in an old tire, but pollution is a serious threat to sea anemones.

Sea anemones are also threatened by changes to the ocean environment. Most anemones live in shallow water near the coastline. These habitats are impacted by increased human development and population growth. Chemicals from pollution can harm the delicate anemones. Pollution also makes the water cloudy. If sunlight cannot penetrate the water, the algae living within the anemone will die. Without their beneficial algae, many anemones would be unable to thrive. Sea anemones are also at risk when the animals they prey on decline due to pollution and overfishing.

Sea anemones are among the most beautiful creatures in the ocean. Their unusual bodies and bright colors are fascinating. Scientists continue to study sea anemones to unlock their many mysteries. For example, studying the venom in nematocysts may lead to new medical treatments for humans. We must protect our oceans so these strange and beautiful creatures can continue to survive.

THINK ABOUT IT

PEOPLE RARELY EAT SEA ANEMONES. WHY DO YOU THINK THIS IS? FIND ANOTHER RESOURCE WITH INFORMATION ABOUT HUMANS EATING SEA ANEMONES.

Learning more about sea anemones may lead to important medical discoveries.

THINK ABOUT IT

- Read chapter 3 again. Describe all the ways in which sea anemones can obtain food. What facts about anemone feeding surprised you the most? Which facts did you already know?

- Sea anemones are closely related to corals. Find some information and close-up pictures of corals and compare the coral colony to a sea anemone. In what ways are these creatures alike? How are they different?

- Chapter 5 mentions research on possible medical uses for nematocyst venom. What would be the benefits of discovering a use for this venom? What might be some potential concerns?

LEARN MORE

FURTHER READING

Fautin, Daphne G., and Gerald R. Allen. *Anemone Fishes and Their Host Sea Anemones*. Minneapolis: Voyageur Press, 1994.

Hirschmann, Kris. *Sea Anemones*. Detroit: KidHaven Press, 2005.

Schaefer, Lola M. *Sea Anemones*. Mankato, MN: Capstone Press, 1998.

WEB SITES

Monterey Bay Aquarium—Videos
www.montereybayaquarium.org/videos/Video.aspx?enc=0ZZ+8rD1FkZFMg4UwjaBnQ
Watch a spectacular video of a giant green sea anemone feeding.

National Wildlife Federation—Kids: Ranger Rick
www.nwf.org/Kids/Ranger-Rick/Animals/Fish/Sea-Anemones.aspx
Read interesting information about and see photographs of anemones.

Sheppard Software—Sea Anemones
www.sheppardsoftware.com/content/animals/animals/invertebrates/seaanemone.htm
This site provides an overview of sea anemone anatomy and biology with pictures and interesting facts.

GLOSSARY

anus (EY-nuss) the opening for the exit of waste materials from digestion

carnivore (KAHR-nuh-vor) an animal that eats other animals

colonial (ka-LONE-ee-uhl) living in a group with individual members connected to each other

cylinder (SIL-uhn-dur) a shape with flat, circular ends and sides shaped like the outside of a tube

nematocyst (NEM-uh-tih-sist) special cells that contain a barbed tube that delivers a paralyzing sting

nudibranchs (NUDE-i-branks) marine snails that lack a shell

pelagic (puh-LA-gik) moving freely in the water by swimming or floating

plankton (PLANGK-tuhn) small aquatic plants and animals that drift in the water

sensory (SEN-suh-ree) able to receive information from the surroundings

shedding (SHED-ing) losing, getting rid of, or letting something fall

sperm (SPURM) male reproductive cell

substrate (SUB-strayt) any firm material that organisms can attach to

tentacles (TEN-tuh-kuhlz) slender, flexible limbs in an animal, used for grasping or moving around, or containing sense organs

venomous (VEN-uhm-uss) having the ability to inflict a poisonous wound

INDEX